Never Use
More Than
Two Different
Typefaces
And 50 other
Ridiculous Typography Rules

COLOPHON

BIS Publishers
Het Sieraad
Postjesweg 1
1057 DT Amsterdam
The Netherlands
T (+) 31 (0)20-515 02 30
F (+) 31 (0)20-515 02 39
bis@bispublishers.nl
www.bispublishers.nl

ISBN 978-90-6369-216-2

Copyright © 2010 BIS Publishers

Ridiculous Design Rules is a concept developed
by Lemon Scented Tea and commissioned by
Premsela, Dutch Platform for Design and Fashion
(www.premsela.org).

Editorial Director: Anneloes van Gaalen
(www.paperdollwriting.com)
Designed by: Lilian van Dongen Torman
(www.born84.nl)

BISPUBLISHERS

Never Use More Than Two Different Typefaces

And 50 other
Ridiculous Typography Rules

CONTENTS

In the world of typography, legibility and readability reign supreme. In an effort to achieve both, designers can rely on a whole list of rules, restrictions and regulations. 'Never Stretch a Font', 'Never Use More Than Two Typefaces', 'Never Use White Type On a Black Background'; the list goes on and on. These design dogmas are helpful tools for typeface rookies, but it's not just the new kids on the typography block that use them.

Ridiculous Typography Rules is the fifth and final book in a series that focuses on rules that people working in the creative industry – graphic designers, fashion designers, advertisers and typographers – can rely on, or ignore entirely, while carrying out their craft. And while experimentation and blatant disregard of the rules are certainly no exception in the typographic field, there are some basic rules that even the most experimental (type) designers stick to, that is, if they want their letters or text to be legible or readable.

This book not only lists 51 rules that govern the world of typography, it also includes the thoughts and opinions of type designers and other creatives, as well as typography and other work that either supports or negates the rules. The aim in making this book was not to create a type bible that lists all the do's and don'ts. Instead, consider it a source of inspiration that hopefully offers some food for thought. In the end, the book is meant to be both an introduction for typographic newbies and a source of reference for font veterans.

Also available in the Ridiculous Design Rules series are *Never Use White Type on a Black Background and 50 other Ridiculous Design Rules*, *Never Leave the House Naked and 50 other Ridiculous Fashion Rules*, *The Medium is the Message and 50 other Ridiculous Advertising Rules* and *Never Use Pop Up Windows and 50 other Ridiculous Web Rules*.

Never use more than two different typefaces

It's the unwritten rule of typography: a document should not feature more than two typeface families - although some typographers take a more lenient approach and draw the line at three.

"There are now about as many different varieties of letters as there are different kinds of fools."
Eric Gill (1882-1940), British sculptor and typeface designer

"Use two typeface families maximum. OK, maybe three."
Timothy Samara, American designer and educator

"A designer should only use these five typefaces: Bodoni, Helvetica, Times Roman, Century, Futura."
Massimo Vignelli (1931), Italian designer

"A single type family with a variety of weights and italics should be enough all by itself; adding a second is nice for texture, but don't overdo it. Too many typefaces are distracting and self-conscious and might confuse or tire the reader."
Timothy Samara, American designer and educator

"Keep this principle in mind: one or two typefaces are enough for any work. You might need three and up to four for complicated and extensive projects like newspapers or magazines, but the base of a publication usually consists of only a couple of typefaces. You don't need more than that."
Enric Jardí (1964), Spanish font and graphic designer

"Conventional wisdom holds that most projects require only three typefaces, or, more precisely, three type families."
Ina Saltz, American art director and designer

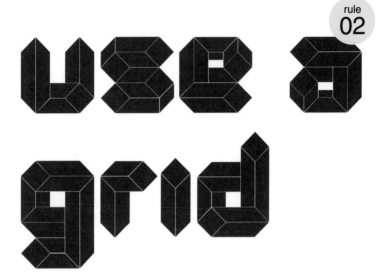

use a grid

The grid: it's the unsung hero of design, which provides both the framework and underlying structure. It's the very foundation of design and therefore a staple in the toolbox of designers, graphic artists and typographers alike.

———

"A design should have some tension and some expression in itself. I like to compare it with the lines on a football field. It is a strict grid. Inside this grid, you play a game, and these can be nice games or very boring games..."
Wim 'Gridnik' Crouwel (1928), Dutch graphic designer and typographer

"Grids do not exist in a vacuum. They exist in relation to the content. We never start with a grid. We start with an idea which is then translated into a form, a structure."
Linda van Deursen (1961), Dutch typographer

"To say a grid is limiting is to say that language is limiting, or typography is limiting. It is up to us to use these media critically or passively."
Ellen Lupton (1963), American graphic designer, writer and curator

"Grids are a very useful invention and they save hours of manual adjusting, but they can become a nuisance. If you completely fix all of the text styles to the grid, you will be clumsily moving the blocks of texts over the page. It is best to adjust texts to grids only when the style truly needs it."
Enric Jardí (1964), Spanish font and graphic designer

"We use grids in our work, but we think we use them in a completely different way than, for example, Swiss late-modernist designers such as Josef Müller-Brockmann. Although we really admire grid-driven work, we wouldn't dare to call ourselves proper Gridniks."
Experimental Jetset (founded in 1997), Dutch graphic design unit

"What might look quite obvious and normal to you when you read your daily paper is the result of careful planning and applied craft. Even newspapers with pages that look messy are laid out following complex grids and strict hierarchies."
Erik Spiekermann and E.M. Ginger, Stop Stealing Sheep & Find Out How Type Works (2003)

"The essential ingredients for good type design: using a grid, and knowing when to forsake it."
Timothy Donaldson, British type designer

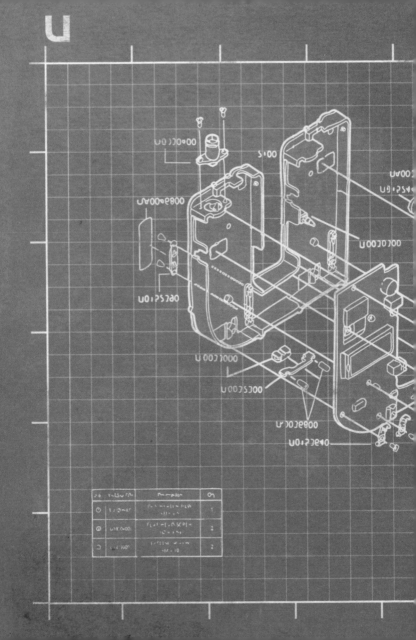

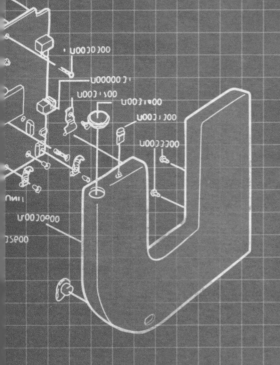

Good type speaks louder than words

Never underestimate the power of good type, British design critic and writer Rick Poynor warns: "Maybe the feeling you have when you see particular typographic choices used on a piece of packaging is just 'I like the look of that, that feels good, that's my kind of product'. But that's the type casting its secret spell."

"Picture yourself in a world without type. True, you could do without some of the ubiquitous advertising messages, but you wouldn't even know which package on your breakfast table contained what."
Erik Spiekermann (1947), German typographer and designer

"A good typeface is well crafted and useful, and sets up into attractive-looking words. It also holds together as a complete system, where individual letters don't distract the reader. A good typeface doesn't make you wonder what you might do with it, or why it exists."
Christian Schwartz (1977), American type designer

"No successful typeface or lettering treatment just *happens*. Before the pencils are sharpened or the computer screen illuminated, there is an idea or concept. A designer understands the content that the letters will communicate and the context in which they will appear. The clearer this perception is, the more precise and powerful the project's results are. A well-developed idea contributes just as much as well-constructed characters to lettering and type's successful outcome."
Bruce Willen and Nolen Strals, authors of Lettering & Type: Creating Letters and Designing Typefaces *(2009)*

There is no such thing as bad type

rule
04

Bad type is what happens when mediocre designers get their hands on good typeface.

———

"There are bad types and good types, and the whole science and art of typography begins after the first category has been set aside."
Beatrice Warde (1900-1969), American typographer, writer and scholar

"Overall, the experience of seeing my typefaces in use has been a good and encouraging one, but there are obviously examples from time to time of a typeface being put in a situation where it has to fail, and that's annoying."
Matthew Carter (1937), British type designer

"My main concern about bad typography is being over-reliant on the computer to solve typographical problems; having the software to distort type in the right hands is a bonus – in the wrong hands, a disaster."
Alan Meeks (1951), British font designer

"Style is a human weakness. There are fonts we think look nice and fonts we think are ugly. We cannot avoid it. There are typefaces and ways of using them that we find appropriate for certain topics and we are sure that they would not work in others, even though we cannot explain it."
Enric Jardí (1964), Spanish font and graphic designer

"If a typeface has qualities that make it fit for even one situation, can it be considered a 'bad' typeface?"
Ina Saltz, American art director and designer

"I think the fear type designers have is that when our typefaces are misused, they make the typefaces look bad and people won't want to use them. In general, I don't worry too much when I see my typefaces looking bad. I think designers remember the good examples of the typefaces they see for longer than the bad examples. That's how it is for me at least. Of course, I can see how in the case of something like Avant Garde, the sheer number of bad examples might overwhelm the good ones. But then you can always draw a new one."
Cyrus Highsmith (1973), American type designer

"In the right hands, technical constraints turn into celebrations of simplicity, and awkward alphabets are typographic heroes for a day. There is no bad type."
Erik Spiekermann and E.M. Ginger, Stop Stealing Sheep & Find Out How Type Works *(2003)*

The Fonts are cool

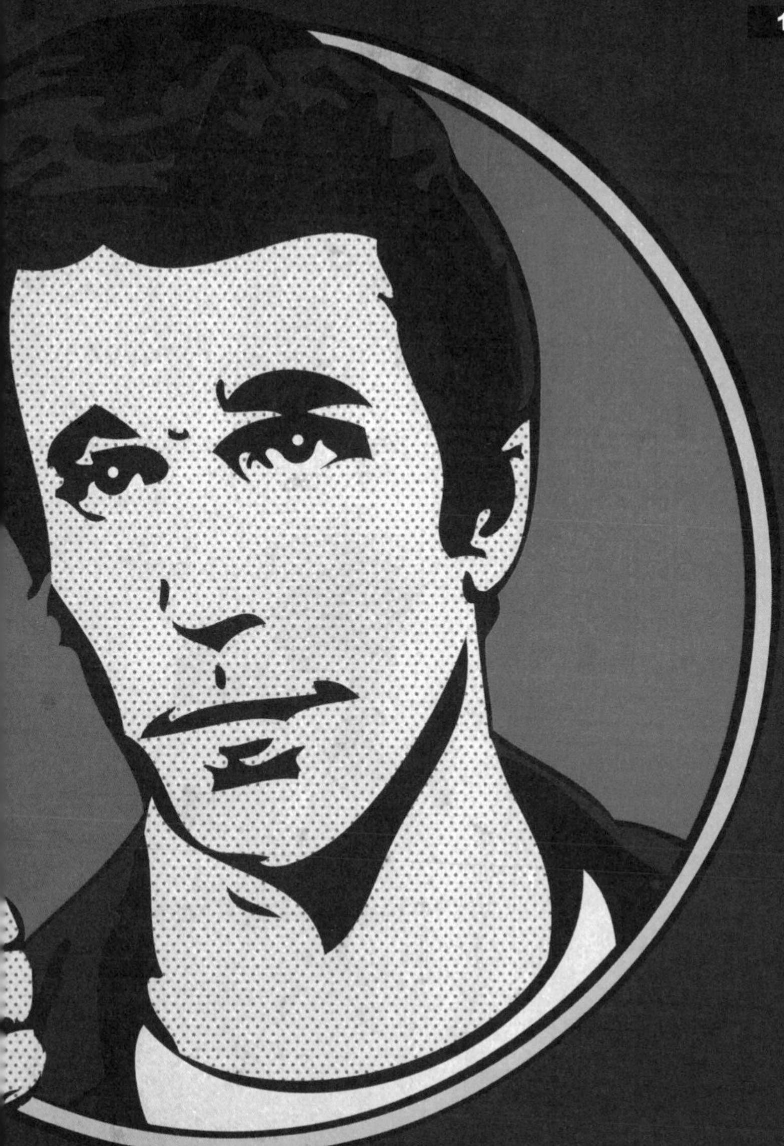

USE ITALICS TO CREATE EMPHASIS

Trying to grab your reader's attention is one thing, but remember to keep it simple. American typographer Allan Haley argues that when it comes to creating emphasis, you want to be discrete: "Emphasis depends on exception. The more things are emphasized, the less effective the emphasis." And if you are going to create emphasis, opt for italics, it's the best, and least obtrusive, option: "The simplest way to create emphasis is to use an italic. Even though italics are generally intended for titles, foreign words, technical terms, and the like, they can also be subtle emphasizers. Using the italic form of a typeface creates a distinct yet harmonious departure in text copy."

———————

"The classic means of giving emphasis to a word or phrase in continuous text is to set it in italic. Common experience suggests that italic is somewhat slower to read than roman type, and its use in large quantities is not appreciated by readers. Used sparingly, it has the advantage of attracting the reader's attention without disturbing the flow of the text."
Jost Hochuli (1935), Swiss typographer and graphic designer

"If you want to invite people to read your texts, make italics and small capital the exception and not the rule."
Enric Jardí (1964), Spanish font and graphic designer

"A conventional rule says that you can't set whole pages, let alone books, in the italics of a typeface. The only reason it might not work is because we're not used to it."
Erik Spiekermann and E.M. Ginger, Stop Stealing Sheep & Find Out How Type Works *(2003)*

THE
ITALIC
POSTER

21

Type design is a discipline

Buying or indeed producing fonts is easier in this new digital day and age but that doesn't turn your run-of-the-mill designer into a typographer. Typography remains a specialized discipline, at least according to type designers.

———————

"Discipline in typography is a prime virtue. Individuality must be secured by means that are rational. Distinction needs to be won by simplicity and restraint. It is equally true that these qualities need to be infused with a certain spirit and vitality, or they degenerate into dullness and mediocrity."
Stanley Morison (1889 -1967), British typographer

"The part discipline plays in experimentation can be likened to the role of improvization in music - before this can happen with any degree of accomplishment, you have to know your instrument inside out."
Jon Wozencroft (1958), British graphic designer

" Ofcourse, type design is a discipline. "

Bruno Maag (1962), Swiss font designer

"Designers are well aware of the values of typography, the only problem is that a lot of them believe that they can design typefaces too! The majority of designers that I know are well educated in the background of typography. I really think there is a problem, though, with the downgrading of type design today. This is due to the freeware fonts that are given away – this really pollutes hard-working type designers who spend years designing a typeface, rather than days. I think designers should be aware of the amount of time it takes to design a typeface."

Nick Hayes, owner of Identikal Foundry

"Type design is a highly specialized discipline. A few dozen type designers create and deliver fonts as semiproducts to a more numerous group of people who use them. You don't need a deep knowledge of type design in order to use fonts, it really depends how you use type. However, designers who make books, printed matter or even Web pages should have some knowledge of typography, as it affects the readability of the material they work with."

Peter Biľak (1973), Slovakian graphic and typeface designer

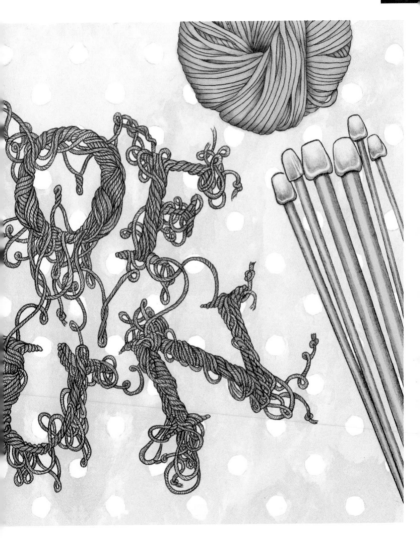

Make it legible

It's the old form versus function debate. Experimenting with form is fine, but at the end of the day the letters you design should still be recognizable and legible.

"Legibility, in practice, amounts simply to what one is accustomed to."
Eric Gill (1882-1940), British sculptor and typeface designer

"I first experienced the power of type to make the whole intellectual world readable with the same letters in the days of metal. This awakened in me the urge to develop the best possible legibility."
Adrian Frutiger (1928), Swiss typeface designer

"One of the principles of durable typography is always legibility: some earned or unearned interest that gives its living energy to the page. It takes various forms and goes by various names, including serenity, liveliness, laughter, grace and joy."
Robert Bringhurst (1946), Canadian poet, typographer, and author

"Legibility, legibility, legibility… Like real estate's mantra (location, location, location), type exists to serve content, so its primary goal should be the ability to invite the reader to apprehend the content."
Ina Saltz, American art director and designer

"Don't confuse legibility with communication. Just because something is legible doesn't mean it communicates and, more importantly, doesn't mean it communicates the right thing."

David Carson (1952), American graphic designer

"Experimentation by its very nature means trying new things. Legibility is dependent on what we're used to reading and so when you introduce something new, it will be less legible, for a while at least."
Bruno Maag (1962), Swiss font designer

"Whatever it is, it must be legible. There is no type without the reader, no font without customers... Then comes art, but it always comes second."
František Štorm (1966), Czech type designer

"A hardly legible headline can attract the reader's interest, while an illegible text will bore him. So the trade is done with that in mind."
Thomas Schostok (1972), German graphic and type designer

"By walking the line between legibility and illegibility you actually catch the viewer's attention."
Lesley Moore (founded in 2004), Dutch graphic design unit

"As in all applied arts, functionality lies at the heart of lettering and typography. Legibility is what makes letterforms recognizable and gives an alphabet letter the ability and power to speak through its shape."
Bruce Willen and Nolen Strals, authors of Lettering & Type: Creating Letters and Designing Typefaces *(2009)*

The quick brown fox jumps over the lazy dog.

Typeface Posters:
soggetto 5 di 5

Typeface Posters fa parte di Lazydog, un progetto per promuovere la grafica pensata e l'innovazione tipografica in Italia.

Typeface Posters belongs to Lazydog, a project meant to promote design culture, good graphic and typography innovation in Italy.

poster #05 — The quick brown fox jumps over the lazy dog.

dimensioni 70x100 cm
size 28x40 inches

stampa digitale su carta Magistri Blueback 135gr
digital print on cage Magistri Blueback paper

cyan + black

Nessun carattere è stato maltrattato durante la composizione di queste poster.

No typefaces were harmed during the typesetting of this poster.

design by lmezeta.it
© 2008 Stefano Johan Lionetti

www.lcindsli.com
www.lazydog.it

Try and error

Trial, error and plenty of patience
are the building blocks for a career in
typography.

―――――――――

"I think there's more to the design
process than simple trial and error,
but errors are often the price paid
for successful trials."
*Matthew Carter (1937), British type
designer*

"I am not sure what an ideal edu-
cation in type looks like. I would say
that I am a believer in an apprentice-
style system, which is how I learned
at Font Bureau. I believe in teaching
a specific method for drawing type and
learning from experience. I think the
best thing someone can do to learn to
draw type is to draw as many different
kinds of typefaces as they can."
*Cyrus Highsmith (1973), American
type designer*

"Drawing type … is a real craft. I've
learned it by doing it a whole lot, and
getting a lot of really terrible work out
of my system early. Self-editing is the
hardest thing to learn."
*Christian Schwartz (1977), American
type designer*

"Mistakes designers make include not
giving the typography enough space
on a page, line lengths that are too long
and hard to read, putting type over a
detailed image so the words become
illegible, using a headline typeface for
body copy, and using all caps in large
blocks of type."
*Martin Fewell, British graphic and
type designer*

Don't let bad spelling hurt great design

rule
09

i was *speach*

"If Al Gore invented the Internet,
I invented spell check."
Dan Quayle (1947), former
American Vice President

"Creating texts with inappropriate
characters is like eating with your
hands: it is not only a question of
manners, but of hygiene as well. A
text with incorrect symbols or errors
in typographical syntax is obscene.
But worse than that, it can lead to
misunderstandings."
Enric Jardí (1964), Spanish font
and graphic designer

ever
ess

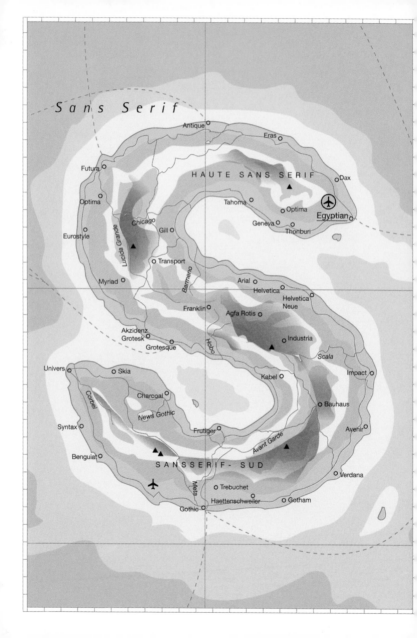

Stick with (sans) serif

To serif or not, that is the question. In general, serifs work well in long texts, while sans serif fonts best serve headings and captions.

"The serif has many purposes and possible origins, and it took some time before I felt ready to handle this item. The serif may carry a burden of out-dated conventions, so applying serifs is risky when trying to avoid the swamp of traditions."
Evert Bloemsma (1958-2005), Dutch type designer

"Mixing serif with sans only makes sense when the serif and the sans type-faces are both derived from the same foundation, or even from the same skeleton. It sounds simple: take a serif design, cut off the serifs, lower the contrast, and there you have a sans serif. But of course there is more to it than that."
Martin Majoor (1960), Dutch type and graphic designer

"Serif typefaces do not usually have good bolds. It is better to replace them with sans serif."
Enric Jardí (1964), Spanish font and graphic designer

"Hey Helvetica – you look disgusting. Have some dignity and put on some serifs."
Stephen Colbert (1964), American comedian and television host

"It would be nice if serif types made a comeback in corporate design. We seem to be in a rut of 'the simple sans', and everyone's re-inventing the same letter. Time to move on."
Jeremy Tankard (1969), British font designer

Good designers copy, great designers steal

Copying is fine; shamelessly ripping off other people's design isn't.

———————

"I am just so tired of people thinking that pirating my typefaces is a form of rebellion. It's not - I am not a big multi-national corporation, I draw the fonts on my own and at present I can't do it full time because I don't make a living out of it. People copy my fonts because they want to steal it and not pay for its usage, nothing more and there is no justification for it. If people want to use them in a charity project or are at college, then fine, I will discuss it, but nobody else has an excuse."
Jonathan Barnbrook (1966), British graphic designer and typographer

"Nothing is original. Steal from anywhere that resonates with inspiration or fuels your imagination. Devour old films, new films, music, books, paintings, photographs, poems, dreams, random conversations, architecture, bridges, street signs, trees, clouds, bodies of water, light and shadows. Select only things to steal from that speak directly to your soul. If you do this, your work (and theft) will be authentic. Authenticity is invaluable; originality is nonexistent. And don't bother concealing your thievery – celebrate it if you feel like it."
Jim Jarmusch (1953), American filmmaker

Never use the spacebar to align text

"Using the spacebar to align text is a recipe for disaster."
Deke McClelland, American author and electronic publishing expert

create a strong hierarchy

Variation in face, color, weight, size, and position: all create a hierarchy and convey to the reader what matters most.

———

"Make the most important information larger or bolder, or set it in another face to distinguish it from less important text. Varying fonts as well as text size and weight can also help set apart different types of material, but keep it simple. If each style doesn't have a clear purpose, many different styles can be confusing."

Beth Tondreau, American designer

"Weightier forms may supersede position and size as a determinant of hierarchy; however, typographic hierarchy is relative, therefore it depends on how weighty versus how big versus how prominently positioned."
Ina Saltz, American art director, author and professor

"Letterers and typographers frequently create hierarchy by mixing display letters with book type."
Bruce Willen and Nolen Strals, authors of Lettering & Type: Creating Letters and Designing Typefaces *(2009)*

"Typography is a journey and your viewer must be taken on one. All journeys have a start and end point to them and your hierarchy should really bring this home; your viewers must be engaged. A typographic piece must have order and structure. All the great typographers of today are very good at this."
Nick Hayes, owner of Identikal Foundry

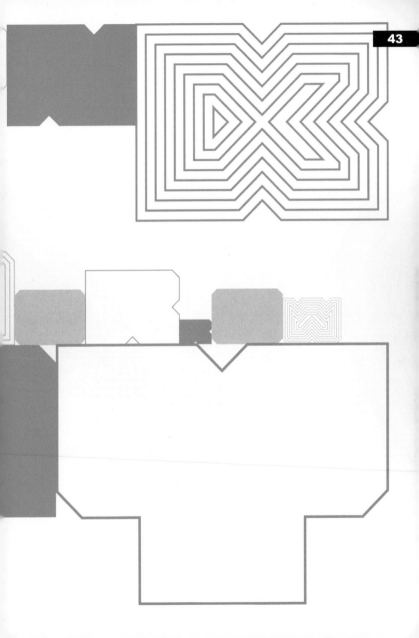

ROMAN CAPITALS

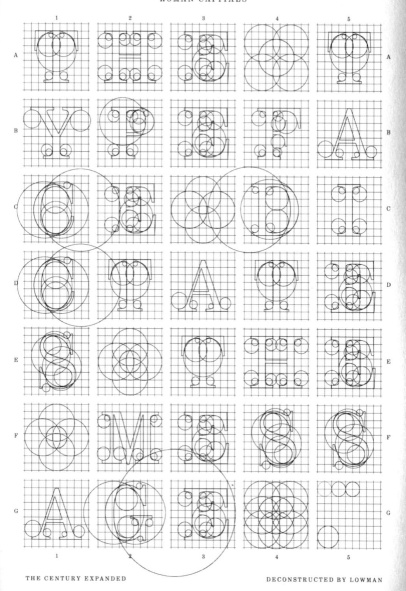

Typeface dictates the message

Typeface conveys meaning, and therefore a message.

"Each face has a spirit of its own. New types express the tempo of the times."
Frederic Goudy (1865-1947), American type designer

"The meaning is in the content of the text and not in the typeface."
Wim 'Gridnik' Crouwel (1928), Dutch graphic designer and typographer

"Typography is a simple way of communicating a message quite unambiguously. And by choosing the right typeface you can add a further, more subliminal message, which the reader will pick up subconsciously."
Bruno Maag (1962), Swiss font designer

"Depending on the style of type, size, leading, spacing, you can alter how the viewer reads information. You can create an image with typography. You can influence opinions with typography."
Bruno Maag (1962), Swiss font designer

"Letters are the throbbing heart of visual communication. For all the talk of the death of print and the dominance of the image, written words remain the engine of information exchange. Text is everywhere. It is a medium and a message. It is a noun and a verb."
Ellen Lupton (1963), American graphic designer, writer and curator

"Good typography always reflects on its contents."
Peter Biľak (1973) Slovakian graphic and typeface designer

"Type is saying things to us all the time. Typefaces express a mood, an atmosphere. They give words a certain coloring."
Rick Poynor, British design writer

rule
14

Don't turn the typeface into an image

Spanish font and graphic designer Enric Jardí argues in his book *Twenty-two Things You Should Never Do With Typeface* that you should never try to convert a typeface into an image, because the typeface is an image in itself: "If you need graphic resources in your design, do not create new images from text. The letters are an image, just as they are."

"I think it is generally agreed that picture writing was the beginning of our lettering. You might wish to communicate something to someone at a distance. If you have no letters, or none common both to you & to your correspondent, what else can you do but draw a picture? The language of pictures is common to all. After a time your pictures are used to signify words and not simply things, and as the system develops and communications become more precise, the pictures become simpler and simpler, more & more conventional, and they come to signify single sounds rather than whole words. And the pictures, by now, have ceased to be pictures. They are, by now, hardly recognizable as representations of things: they are conventional signs, & their pictorial origin is forgotten."
Eric Gill (1882-1940), British sculptor and typeface designer

SHINIER
SHINIER
SHINI
YOUNGER
BIGGER N BIGGER
TANNED
BIGGER
YOUNGER
SLEEKER

"One of the joys of working with letterforms is their uncanny ability to be shaped into images. For designers who enjoy 'playing,' typographic forms in all of their infinite variations are like a gigantic set of Legos, building blocks that allow us to create images that speak to viewers both as visuals and as text."
Ina Saltz, American art director, author and professor

"I like integrating lettering into the image of the poster so that it really feels like one whole thing… Sometimes I'll focus my energy more on the information, the letters than the image – making the letters into the image themselves."
Shaun Flynn, American musician and artist

"As letterforms transform into pattern or imagery, their text can become extremely difficult to decipher. Not everyone finds this problematic. What a designer loses in legibility might be recovered through the heightened graphic or narrative importance of the letters."
Bruce Willen and Nolen Strals, authors of Lettering & Type: Creating Letters and Designing Typefaces *(2009)*

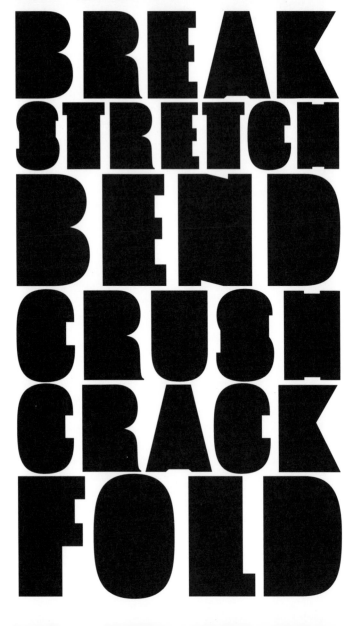

Never stretch a font

The third volume of *Indie Fonts* notes that there is nothing wrong with "compressing (or stretching) a font within its capacity." But stretch it any further and you're in trouble: "The problem arises when a font has been compressed [or stretched] beyond its ability to retain a pleasing and readable effect."

―――――

"A lot of screen companies only make their fonts look good for one particular size, but then they totally change their character when they get bigger or smaller."
Erik Spiekermann (1947), German typographer and designer

"When it comes to type and type usage, never stretch a font beyond its boundaries. Don't modify something to the point where it looks distorted. When that happens, the reader doesn't notice the message before he notices the oddity. You don't want the type to catch the attention of the reader's eye more than the message."
Dennis Ortiz-Lopez, American typography designer

Good typeface is invisible

To quote the famed American type designer Frederic W. Goudy (1865-1947): "The perfect type would be completely invisible."

"Type design moves at the pace of the most conservative reader. The good type-designer therefore realizes that, for a new font to be successful, it has to be so good that only very few recognize its novelty."
Stanley Morison (1889-1967), British typographer

"Type well used is invisible as type, just as the perfect talking voice is the unnoticed vehicle for the transmission of words, ideas."
Beatrice Warde (1900-1969), American typographer, writer and scholar

"The most important thing I have learned is that legibility and beauty stand close together and that type design, in its restraint, should be only felt but not perceived by the reader."
Adrian Frutiger (1928), Swiss typeface designer

"I am convinced that people recognize good typography but do not know why. Given two samples – one good, one bad – they would be hard pushed to distinguish between the two, but subliminally would recognize the difference without knowing why and always prefer the good."
Alan Meeks (1951), British font designer

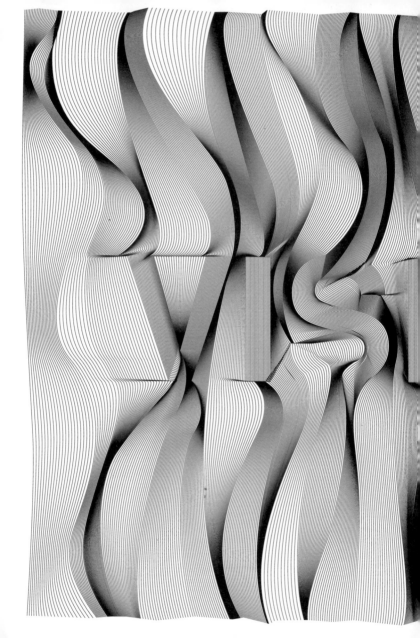

THINKING
made
visual

"Design is thinking made visual"

rule
18

"Typography at its best is a visual form
of language linking timelessness and time."

*Robert Bringhurst (1946),
American poet, typographer and author*

This well-known design mantra was coined by American graphic designer and filmmaker Saul Bass (1920-1996), best known for his title sequences and film posters.

———

"Typographical design should perform optically what the speaker creates through voice and gesture of his thoughts."
El Lizzitsky (1890-1941), Russian artist and designer

"I'm very much a word person, so that's why typography for me is the obvious extension. It just makes my words visible."
Erik Spiekermann (1947), German typographer and designer

"When a client comes to a designer – to any creative – it's not just the output; it's about the person: the way they think and the way they approach the work ... and that only comes from thinking."
Ian Coyle, American strategist and designer

"Typography is as important as ever – how else do you visualize words?"
Bruno Maag (1962), Swiss font designer

Make it readable

In the world of typography, legibility and readability reign supreme. And rightly so. After all, you want people to be able to see and read the words in front of them.

———————

"There are essentially two kinds of typography: the familiar kind for reading, and the other, simply for viewing, like a painting. Some say that readability is most important. There are really two important things about typography: readability and beauty; both are equally important. However, many readable typefaces are visually offensive. The design of a typeface, ugly or not, is only one aspect of the problem of readability. How a typeface is used is equally, if not more, important."
Paul Rand (1914-1996), American graphic designer

"The readability of a text is influenced not only by the choice of typeface, type size, correct or incorrect letter- and wordspacing, and the length of line, but also linespacing or interlinear space, often termed 'leading'."
Jost Hochuli (1935), Swiss typographer and graphic designer

"The most popular typefaces are the easiest to read; their popularity has made them disappear from conscious cognition. It becomes impossible to tell if they are easy to read because they are commonly used, or if they are commonly used because they are easy to read."
Zuzana Licko (1961), Slovakian type designer

"Remember, type is there to be read."
Enric Jardí (1964), Spanish font and graphic designer

A PICTURE IS WORTH A THOUSAND WORDS

rule
20

A picture might be worth a thousand words, but good type speaks louder than anything and can, in the words of American art director Nancy Harris Rouemy, even "transmit a message that a photograph or classic illustration cannot."

"As the Chinese say, 1001 words is worth more than a picture."
John McCarthy (1927), American computer scientist

"A picture says more than a thousand words, only as much as a thousand words say more than a picture. A thousand apples don't taste any better than a pear, and a thousand pears don't taste any better than an apple. The apple tastes different from the pear, no matter how many of them there are. A thousand words say something different from a picture"
Bo Bergström (1946), Swedish author, lecturer and creative director

"Typography is an art form, but it's an art form directly related to its function – and the primary function of typography is to be read. The importance of any campaign is to get the message across, and this is better achieved by words rather than image."
Alan Meeks (1951), British font designer

"Typography is still as important as ever. In some situations, probably more so, as images can be interpreted in more ways than one, while text communicates directly. It would be a brave shop to just put up a blank red banner at sale time; it seems obligatory that the white 'sale' word should appear too."
Jeremy Tankard (1969), British font designer

"Readers want to meet the face or place or thing that is described in the story, and there is no doubt that photographs establish an objective reality for the content. But every so often, type transmits a message that a photograph or classic illustration cannot."
Nancy Harris Rouemy, American designer and art director

"We need good typography now more than ever; graphic design is words and pictures. You can rarely communicate precisely with images alone, but there are many fine examples of typographic designers spending entire careers achieving accurate and beautiful communication with barely an image."
Timothy Donaldson, British type designer

Never use all CAPS

Try to convey your enthusiasm or the importance of your words in a different way, going all caps is almost never the answer when it comes to creating emphasis.

"NEVER use CAPITAL letters to accentuate words in running copy. They STICK OUT far too much, spoiling the LOOK of the column or page. Use italics instead. If you have to set words in capitals, use proper small caps with or without initial capitals."
Erik Spiekermann (1947), German typographer and designer

"The system of capitalization of letters is a practical rule that is recommendably followed, just as it is best to walk to the right if you do not want to be dodging everyone who comes your way. It is a code agreed upon by everyone, though it is not a crime to break the rules, either."
Enric Jardí (1964), Spanish font and graphic designer

"Perpetrators of proper crimes against linguistics should be tried, convicted and locked inside a dusty moth-ridden library with a set of dictionaries until they start coming out with proper sentences again. After rehabilitation, an alarm should go off when they touch caps lock, while a colon and bracket pressed in quick succession should delete all the text they'd previously written."
Ariane Sherine (1980), British comedy writer and journalist

"Do not forgo the liberal use of capitals within your text, for the geometric letterforms can provide some diabolically good outcomes."
Paul Felton (1984), British graphic designer

"If you really want to aggravate someone, using all caps is an effective way to do it. A study of email users in the United States and Britain found that overuse of capitals was the thing that most irritated email recipients."
David Shipley and Will Schwalbe, American authors of Send: The Essential Guide to Email for Office and Home *(2007)*

"Design is a problem-solving activity."

"Design is a problem-solving activity."
A design mantra that comes courtesy of
American graphic designer Paul Rand
(1914-1996).

"Of course design is about problem
solving, but I cannot resist adding
something personal."
*Wim Crouwel (1928), Dutch graphic
designer and typographer*

"Design is directed toward human
beings. To design is to solve human
problems by identifying them, exam-
ining alternate solutions to them,
choosing and executing the best solution."
*Ivan Chermayeff (1932), American
graphic designer*

"I don't solve problems, I create
possibilities."
*Richard Hutten (1967), Dutch
designer*

"Solving problems and working within constraints is what separates real
communication design from making
pretty pictures – in any media. "
*Erik Spiekermann and E.M. Ginger,
Stop Stealing Sheep & Find Out How
Type Works (2003)*

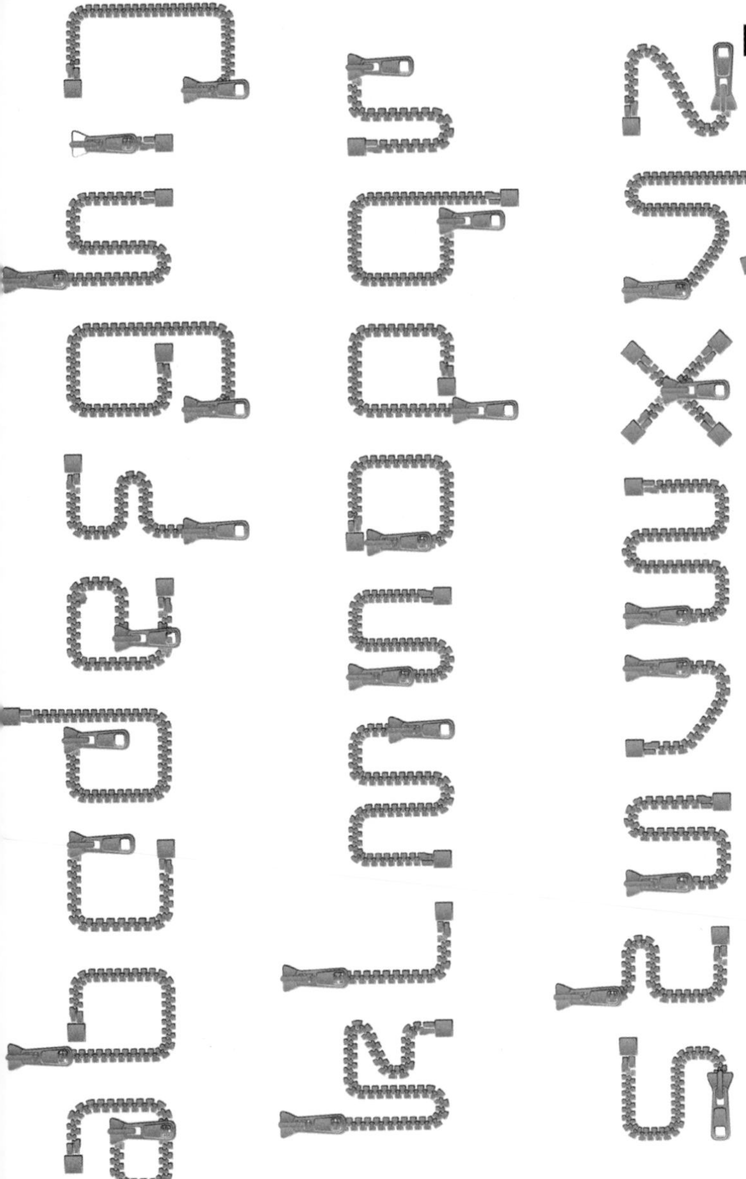

Never use an image behind your text

rule
23

Don't let anything come between you and your text.

———

"Legibility issues come into play when type overlaps images: the image demands our attention."
Ina Saltz, American art director and designer

"When you have a fabulous photo, don't wreck it. Sometimes the best solution is to make a photo as large as possible, crop very little or avoid cropping altogether, and leave the image free of surprinted type or graphic gimmicks."
Beth Tondreau, American designer

Consider the medium

Print, screen, billboard: different mediums call for different type.

———

"Times New Roman was designed for printing a newspaper, Helvetica for advertising. If you can't or won't use software that embeds your own fonts into the web page, at least use Cascading Style Sheets with fonts made for the screen, such as Verdana and Georgia, or bitmap fonts."
Erik Spiekermann (1947), German typographer and designer

"A type designer must know how type works in a piece of text; he must know what happens with type on different sorts of paper; he must know how a typeface behaves with different printing techniques."
Martin Majoor (1960), Dutch type and graphic designer

"Almost all typefaces were devised for a specific medium. Always bear in mind how the one you have chosen will be reproduced... Although at times, typefaces have been used primarily in different media from that they were meant for, it is better not to break this rule; for your design to look good, think about how it will be reproduced. Think about whether the type will appear on newsprint, on a computer screen, on vinyl, or on glossy paper. Think about whether it will be printed on an offset printer, whether it will be painted by hand, or if it will be reproduced by screen printing."
Enric Jardí (1964), Spanish font and graphic designer

"How and where letterforms appear should be a clue as to a designer's typographic decisions; the medium may dictate what constitutes a more legible type choice. Broadly speaking, is the text on a reflective surface (i.e. paper, billboard, truck panel, environmental signage) or a light-emitting surface (i.e. a computer screen, a video screen, a rear verprojection)?"
Ina Saltz, American art director and designer

"There are a multitude of fonts designed with various intentions or purposes. You can see that Verdana was designed for the screen, and some of its details are rather clumsy when used in print in larger sizes. Other fonts like Times work better in print because they were made for it, and suffer on screen. To get most of them, it's good to know a bit about the fonts you use, and ask a few questions: for which medium was the font designed, is it working well with the language I use? Is it intended for small sizes or display use?"
Peter Biľak (1973), Slovakian graphic and typeface designer

"As far as choosing an appropriate typeface goes, don't use a typeface that was designed mainly for screen use (Chicago, Verdana, Lucida) for print (or at least, think really hard about it); conversely (although less problematic) don't use a typeface that was designed for printing a fine art catalogue on your website. There are, of course, some stunning exceptions to the rules here: two of our finest text faces were designed for signs: Frutiger (big airport) and Gill (small bookshop)."
Timothy Donaldson, British type designer

Baskerville

YES   NO

HUMANISTIC FORMS PLEASE YOUR EYE?

OKAY TO A QUESTION OF FOOD

Syntax

GOUDA   EMMENTAL

FF Scala

Joanna

ARE YOU COMPLETELY IN DOUBT?

Minion

BOOK

GOOD   BAD

WHAT IS YOUR OPINION OF ERIC GILL

YES   NO

A CHAMPION IN USABILITY, PERHAPS?

EVERYBODY LOVES GARAMOND

Optima

YES   NO

SO YOU WANT A SANS SERIF, IS THAT THE CASE?

YES   NO

Sabon

OK

HERE WE HAVE A CLASSIC WAITING FOR YOU

BUT PERHAPS ONE WOULD WANT A LARGER EYE?

YES

NO

Garamond

YES

NO

GOT A WHOLE BUNCH OF OFFICE CORRESPONDENCE

GOOD

BAD

HOW DO THE WORDS SEMI-SANS, SEMI-SERIF SOUND?

GOOD

BAD

SOMETHING NEW, GOT SANS?

INVITATION

IS IT AN ITALIAN RESTAURANT?

YES   NO

Zapfino

YES

Rotis

FF Erikrighthaud

NO

LIKE SOMETHING HANDWRITTEN, DO YOU?

YES   NO

Palatino

SOMETHING CALLIGRAPHIC, MAYBE?

HOW ABOUT SOMETHING FANCY?

Lexicon

Walbaum

YES

Bodoni

THIN HAIRLINES

YES

Fedra

Didot

NO

READABILITY?

THINNER HAIRLINES

SOME T

GOT A LOT OF TABLES, HAVE YOU?

YES   NO

WE ALL LIKE SOMETHING CONDENSED, YES?

YES   NO

INFOGRAPHIC

Letter Go

BOOK

Caslo

SO YOU
A TYP

Start out by choosi
that you'll need

(S)pace yourself

"If the spaces are wrong, it doesn't matter what typeface it is, the whole thing will look bad," warns British type designer Timothy Donaldson. So by all means: watch your tracks.

"Anyone who would letterspace lowercase would steal sheep."
Frederic Goudy (1865-1947), American type designer

"Look at the spaces, not just the type."
Alan Meeks (1951), British font designer

"Type designers consider the space between the letters as important as the forms of the letters themselves... A page of text is not only black lines on a white field but also a white space punctuated by black forms. Adjusting the side bearings of each letter orchestrates this interplay between positive and negative space, ultimately defining how a font looks, feels, and works."
Bruce Willen and Nolen Strals, authors of Lettering & Type: Creating Letters and Designing Typefaces *(2009)*

"Do not add extra space between lower-case letters. Unless you have a good reason for it, do not apply more tracking than necessary between lower-case letters."
Enric Jardí (1964), Spanish font and graphic designer

"Drawing is what I always loved the most. I discovered drawing type is drawing in a very pure form. Because a type designer does not draw letters. A type designer designs words, and words are structures that contain patterns of black and white shapes, form and counter form. It is a game that deals with space and rhythm. Which is precisely what, for me, is the essence of drawing."
Cyrus Highsmith (1973), American type designer

CONTRAST BETWEEN TYPE AND BACKGROUND

Use sufficient contrast between type and background. That is, if you want people to be able to read the words and letters you so carefully designed.

"When working with type and color, ensure that sufficient contrast exists between type and its background. Too little contrast in hue, value or saturation, or a combination of these factors, can result in type that is difficult, if not impossible, to read. Be careful when using photos or texture behind text."
Rob Carter (1949), American professor of typography and graphic design

"The difference between foreground and background totality is a key factor in legibility… As type color and background color come closer together in hue, saturation, and density, legibility is reduced."
Ina Saltz, American art director and designer

freehand is obsolete

rule

27

In this high-tech day and age, the tools and means are available for one and all to create picture-perfect type. But perfection is boring. And so, in recent years, there has been a renewed interest in handwritten type, which reveals the maker's mark and unique signature.

"Letters that look like handwriting can be a nice decorative resource, but they are not exactly typefaces."

Enric Jardí (1964), Spanish font and graphic designer

"In our increasingly technical world, there has been a huge backlash against the machine-made aesthetic. Handmade forms appeal to our humanity, and the enormous popularity of handmade objects reflects the do-it-yourself spirit of our time."

Ina Saltz, American art director and designer

"Hand type may not always be the right answer or the most time-effective solution, but it is definitely the most fun. It's the answer I go to most often. It shapes my work and the work of so many around me. It's the answer that keeps the artist from taking himself or herself too seriously and infuses some fun into an industry that sometimes takes itself too seriously. It reveals the hand of the maker, and its viewer finds comfort in that: the artist illustrated by lines made crooked from too many cups of coffee."

Mike Perry, American typographer and graphic designer

"Hand-drawn letters not only convey the content of a particular message, but also have the potential to become the content itself."

Ken Barber, letterer and type designer

"What's more unexpected, more surprising, than someone's handwriting? The best casual typefaces have always managed to carry some of the spontaneity of handwritten letters into the mechanical restrictions of typesetting."
Erik Spiekermann and E.M. Ginger,
Stop Stealing Sheep & Find Out How Type Works *(2003)*

"Handwriting can convey the delicacy and sophistication of a formal cursive, the relaxed timbre of a quick note, or the shakiness of a lunatic scrawl. When written deliberately, handwriting operates much like a palette of fonts. Slight variations in style can express different tones while maintaining the consistency of the writer's hand. Although lettering and type can also evoke personality and mood, handwriting adds an intimacy that the others cannot."
Bruce Willen and Nolen Strals,
authors of Lettering & Type: Creating Letters and Designing Typefaces *(2009)*

Helvetica always works

These days the clean-cut typeface, which was designed back in 1957, seems more popular than ever thanks in part to Lars Müller's book *Helvetica: Homage to a Typeface* and the feature-length documentary by Gary Hustwit which have both travelled the globe.

———————

"You can say, 'I love you', in Helvetica. And you can say it with Helvetica Extra Light if you want to be really fancy. Or you can say it with the Extra Bold if it's really intensive and passionate, you know, and it might work."
Massimo Vignelli (1931), Italian designer

"Helvetica is like a good screwdriver; a reliable, efficient, easy-to-use tool. But put it in the wrong hands, and it's potentially lethal."
Tom Geismar (1931), American designer

"It's air, you know. It's just there. There's no choice. You have to breathe, so you have to use Helvetica."
Erik Spiekermann (1947), German typographer and designer

"Most people who use Helvetica use it because it's ubiquitous. It's like going to McDonald's instead of thinking about food. Because it's there, it's on every street corner, so let's eat crap because it's on the corner."
Erik Spiekermann (1947), German typographer and designer

"I think I'm right calling Helvetica the perfume of the city. It is just something we don't notice usually but we would miss very much if it wouldn't be there."
Lars Müller (1955), Norwegian graphic designer and publisher

"[Helvetica] is all around us. You've probably already seen Helvetica several times today. It might have told you which subway platform you needed, or tried to sell you investment services or vacation getaways in the ads in your morning paper. Maybe it gave you the latest headlines on television, or let you know whether to 'push' or 'pull' to open your office door."
Gary Hustwit (1964), American filmmaker and director of "Helvetica"

"Helvetica maybe says everything, and that's perhaps part of its appeal."
Jonathan Hoefler (1970), American typeface designer

"What we find interesting about Helvetica is its paradoxical nature: on the one hand, it is a neutral typeface, or better said, it is perceived as such. On the other hand, it carries this very heavy ideological baggage. There is this really interesting tension between its functionality, and the meaning that it gained over the years. It is a typeface that is empty and loaded at the same time."
Experimental Jetset (founded in 1997), Dutch graphic design unit

etica

Avoid combining similar typefaces

rule 29

If you want to combine multiple typefaces, which in itself is an issue of typographic debate, at least make sure they aren't too similar. Forgo all subtlety and go for great contrasts instead. After all, opposites attract.

"Do not mix Caslon with Garamond. Do not mix Futura with Helvetica. Do not mix Didot with Walbaum. Do not mix Frutiger with DIN. Do not mix Baskerville with Times. Do not mix Akzidenz with Franklin Gothic. Using typefaces that are too similar is like wearing a sienna sweater and beige pants or ordering two scoops of ice cream, orange and tangerine."
Enric Jardí (1964), Spanish font and graphic designer

"Mixing many typefaces works best when there are extreme differences in the type choices; this implies intent and control underlying the mishmash."
Ina Saltz, American art director and designer

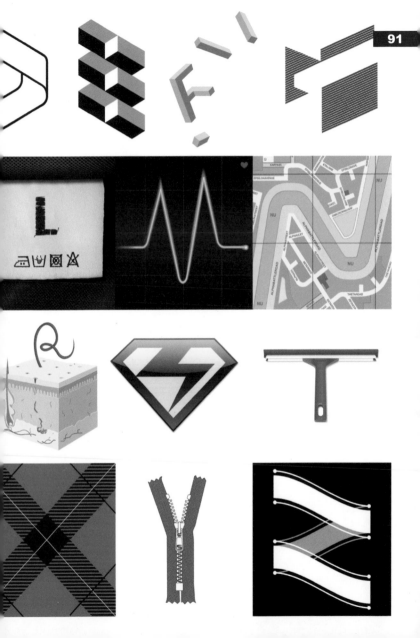

Never use Comic Sans

If you are of the opinion that Helvetica always works, chances are you also believe that Comic Sans never does. This frivolous-looking type has something of a bad rep amongst typographers. It seems to be universally despised: there is even a movement devoted entirely to the eradication of Comic Sans. But it is by no means the first type to suffer this treatment. As Ina Saltz points out, "type is a matter of taste" and tastes change: "in the ninth century, uncials were described as ugly; in the eighteenth century, Bodoni was ridiculed."

"If you love it, you don't know much about typography. If you hate it, you really don't know much about typography, either, and you should get another hobby."
Vincent Connare (1960), American font designer responsible for Comic Sans

"If you design *The Divine Comedy* to be written in Comic Sans, you might be the first one to do it, but you can be sure that that is a wrong decision, inefficient and, as a last resort, just plain tacky. Comic Sans is readable enough to be used in a long text; that is not the problem. The problem is that nobody is going to like it."
Enric Jardí (1964), Spanish font and graphic designer

"Designers hate Comic Sans, for it undercuts the sanctity of their craft... Designing a font for a children's program, Mr Connare plundered comic books (the sans bit refers to sans serif - without flourishes on the end of letters) and an epidemic began. Often wrongly used (on tombstones, of all places), it can be a welcome break from those corporate Arials and oh-so-chic Helveticas."
Editorial in The Guardian *(2009)*

"We believe in the gospel message 'ban comic sans'. It shall be salvation to all who are literate. By banding together to eradicate this font from the face of the earth, we strive to ensure that future generations will be liberated from this epidemic and never suffer this scourge that is the plague of our time."
Manifesto of the Ban Comic Sans movement

Type needs rhythm

Music and typography have more in common than meets the eye. After all, both musical and typographic composition require balance, space and of course rhythm.

"When a type design is good, it is not because each individual letter of the alphabet is perfect in form, but because there is a feeling of harmony and unbroken rhythm that runs through the whole design, each letter kin to every other and to all."

Frederic Goudy (1865-1947),
American type designer

"Rhythm is certainly also a visual term. Yet when we look at visual qualities from another standpoint – the vantage point of music – we gain a fresh insight for applying rhythm to design."
Kenneth Hiebert (1930), American graphic designer

"A real typeface needs rhythm, needs contrast, it comes from handwriting, and that's why I can read your handwriting, you can read mine. And I'm sure our handwriting is miles away from Helvetica or anything that would be considered legible, but we can read it, because there's a rhythm to it, there's a contrast to it."
Erik Spiekermann (1947), German typographer and designer

or

50

ABCDEFGHI
JKLMNOOPQ
STUVVWXYZ

FIND A GOOD BALANCE

rule
32

Balance and proportion. According to British font designer Alan Meeks (1951), these two elements form the basis of all typographic design: "What makes good typography today is what has always made good typography – balance and proportion. If each character is sympathetically balanced with the one next to it, then each word is balanced with the one next to it, then each line and so on. The letters and words should become patterns on the page, and the more attractive and balanced the patterns, the more likely people are to read it."

"Space is visually subdivided by the tension that develops between an element and the boundaries of the space."
Willi Kunz (1943), Swiss graphic designer and typographer

"A typographic piece must be easy on the eye. A viewer can be distracted if they feel uneasy about the balance. Balance and co-ordination are important to the way your hierarchy is read; without them your piece will fall apart."
Nick Hayes, owner of Identikal Foundry

"Space in typography is like time in music. It is infinitely divisible, but a few proportional intervals can be much more useful than a limitless choice of arbitrary quantities."
Robert Bringhurst (1946), Canadian poet, typographer and author

Stick to the basics

Rules are meant to be broken, but before you can even think about breaking the rules of typography, you had better master the basics.

"Stick to the basics. The fundamentals of lettering have endured for a reason, and they still apply in most instances."
Ken Barber, letterer and type designer

"Good typography can be achieved by following some basic rules. As far as type is concerned, the letter shapes need to be harmonious to each other, and well proportioned. A text typeface is to be read, not to be seen. Setting the type with appropriately generous leading and spacing will aid legibility. Using proper quotation marks and the correct dashes all contribute to successful typography."
Bruno Maag (1962), Swiss font designer

"Mastering the art of arranging letters in space and time is essential knowledge for anyone who crafts communications for page or screen."
Ellen Lupton (1963), American graphic designer, writer and curator

"A plea to young designers – learn the basics, then your work will have the underlying authority to be subversive."
Jonathan Barnbrook (1966), British graphic designer and typographer

"When you learn the rules and have had a little practice, nothing will upset you, not in traffic and not in typography."
Erik Spiekermann and E.M. Ginger, Stop Stealing Sheep & Find Out How Type Works (2003)

"Either consciously or unconsciously, type designers build and follow rules that direct the myriad choices involved in creating a font."
Bruce Willen and Nolen Strals, authors of Lettering & Type: Creating Letters and Designing Typefaces (2009)

BIGGER

IS

BETTER

rule
34

When it comes to typography: size matters.

———————

"Bigger isn't always better, but it does get more attention. Size, especially when combined with a more prominent position (i.e. top), is a simple but effective way to emphasize a letterform. Even a modest change in scale can make a big difference."
Ina Saltz, American art director and designer

"In fact, recognizability and readability largely depend on the top half of most characters. So perhaps enhancing this half can have a positive effect on readability."
Evert Bloemsma (1958-2005), Dutch type designer

"'Make it bigger' seems like a logical guideline for creating typographic emphasis. While this can be effective, there are also some potential drawbacks to just bumping up the point size. First, unless you are setting copy with generous line spacing, the bigger type will appear cramped between the lines of type above and below it."
Allan Haley, American typographer

Avoid widows and orphans

rule
35

Don't leave them hanging.

—————

"Avoiding widows and orphans in a text is simply an aesthetic issue, as is eliding articles, pronouns, or short words at the ends of lines or leaving letters alone at the end of unjustified compositions."
Enric Jardí (1964), Spanish font and graphic designer

"A good typographic 'color' on the

page is interrupted when a word or word fragment is alone on a line at the end of a paragraph or column (known as a widow) or, even worse, at the top of a column or page (known as an orphan). The reason an orphan is even worse than a widow is that it not only creates a gap in typographic color, but it also disrupts the horizontal alignment across the tops of the columns of text."
Ina Saltz, American art director and designer

"Don't try to be original, just try to be good."

rule
36

Words of wisdom, once uttered by American graphic designer Paul Rand (1914-1996), who in turn paraphrased German-born American architect Mies van der Rohe (1886-1969).

———

"Originality is a product, not an intention."
Paul Rand (1914-1996), American graphic designer

"Sometimes there is simply no need to be either clever or original."
Ivan Chermayeff (1932), American graphic designer

"Developing authentic and original ideas demands careful observation of, and response to, technological, social, and environmental changes. It also requires independent thinking that is attuned to evolving attitudes and fresh experiences rather than cursory glances through history books and design annuals."
Willi Kunz (1943), Swiss graphic designer and typographer

"Legibility may be slightly compromised in favor of originality or impact, but the legibility should never be allowed to threaten the original creation."
Alan Meeks (1951), British font designer

"Designing in pursuit of being original, or even interesting, can be a foolhardy prospect. Design that strives to be original for the sake of it, and typically at the expense of its real purpose of communication, often falls into a mire of stylistic tropes and shallow meanings."
Jason Santa Maria (1978), American graphic designer

Striving for pretty is one thing, but remember that beauty is in the eye of the beholder and that you can't please all of your type's beholders, all of the time.

"A great typeface is not a collection of beautiful letters, but a beautiful collection of letters."
Walter Tracy (1914–1995), British typographer and designer

rule
37

"Without aesthetic, design is either the humdrum repetition of familiar clichés or a wild scramble for novelty. Without the aesthetic, the computer is but a mindless speed machine, producing effects without substance. Form without relevant content, or content without meaningful form."
Paul Rand (1914-1996), American graphic designer

"My aim in regard to aesthetics is to produce a beautiful piece of design work. A typeface that is good enough to be appreciated as quality craftsmanship."
Bruno Maag (1962), Swiss font designer

"You want beautiful words, not beautiful letters."
Mario Feliciano (1969), Portugese graphic designer

In his 'Ten Commandments of
Typography', British graphic designer
Paul Felton preaches the Gospel of
Type. The Eighth Commandment?
"Thou shalt always align letters and
words on a baseline." Amen.

Hold the (base)line

rule
38

"I have my tricks and habits, I suppose. Looking at things upside down is helpful."

Cyrus Highsmith (1973),
font designer

"Abandon mathematical precision and fall back on optical alignment. That is, move the type until it looks right to your eye … Print out the result on your laser printer and try to evaluate the headline as a set of shapes instead of a series of connected letters. Squint at it. Turn it upside down. Hold it out at arm's length. Prop it up on your desk and step back for a look."
Steve Morgenstern, author of
No-Sweat Desktop Publishing (1992)

"If you turn things upside down, you quickly realise what works and what doesn't."
Siebe Tettero (1958), Dutch architect and designer of Viktor & Rolf's upside-down store

Turn it upside down

A trick of the trade taught by graphic design teachers at schools and colleges the world over.

''You can't turn a thing upside down if there's no theory about it being the right way up.''
Gilbert Keith Chesterton (1874-1936), British writer

''Look at it upside down, in a mirror and reversed out, even add colour or shadow or outline until the basic type looks correct in black & white.''
Alan Meeks (1951), British font designer

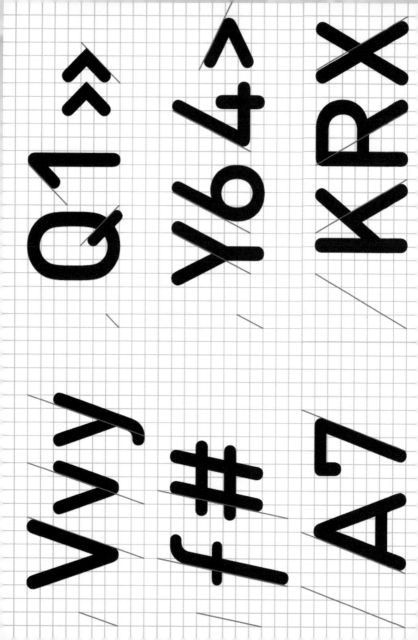

God is in the details

German-born architect Ludwig Mies van der Rohe (1886-1969) usually gets credited for coming up with this rule, although credit should probably go to Gustave Flaubert (1821-80), who said: "Le bon Dieu est dans le détail."

"The details are not the details. They make the design."
Charles Eames (1907-1978),
American architect, graphic and
industrial designer

"Discipline is the god of design that governs every aspect of a project, be it two-, three-, or four-dimensional. 'God is in the details', said Mies van der Rohe. And he was right."
Massimo Vignelli (1931), Italian
designer

"To get it right, you need to look at and question every detail. More often than not, this work is grounded on good foundations. Typesetting used to be carried out by highly skilled individuals. The fine details of typography is a vast area of minute details. Typographers take a great pride in attaining high levels of work. Don't let the computer make the decisions for you!"
Jeremy Tankard (1969), British font
designer

"[Designers that care about type] possess the attention to detail that is required for good typography and they naturally allow that to flow into the rest of their work. 'Design from the word up,' as Mr Spiekermann would say."
Timothy Donaldson, British type
designer

Left
is more.

Typeface Posters:
soggetto 3 di 5

Typeface Posters fa parte di Lazydog, un progetto
per promuovere la grafica pensata e l'innovazione
tipografica in Italia.

*Typeface Posters belongs to Lazydog, a project meant to
promote design culture, good graphic and typography
innovation in Italy.*

poster 105 — Left is more.

dimensione 70x100 cm
size 28x40 inches

stampa digitale su carta Magistra Bluxback 135gr
digital print on 135gr Magistra Bluxback paper

Pantone® 360 + **black**

Nessun carattere è stato maltrattato durante
la composizione di questo poster.

*No typefaces were harmed during the typesetting
of this poster.*

design by zanellili

© 2008 Stefano Joker Lionetti

www.lazydog.it

Align left

Align your text left — that is, when you're dealing with a language where the words are read left to right.

"In a perfect world, all texts should be unjustified and range left. This statement might seem a bit extreme but, if you think about it, setting lines without justifying them is the only way to achieve the optimum space between letters and words."
Enric Jardí (1964), Spanish font and graphic designer

"Less common forms of alignment are fine when used with limited quantities of text."
Ina Saltz, American art director and designer

KNOW YOUR AUDIENCE

rule
42

"THE TYPEFACES USED NEED TO REFLECT THE BRAND YOU'RE WORKING ON."

Martin Fewell, British graphic and type designer

It's not just the medium and the message that dictate the typeface. The people that read the message and see the medium are of equal importance when it comes to choosing type.

———

"The criteria for choosing a typeface are many and varied. You need to consider the mood, target audience, size of eventual usage, and the amount of words to be used. Often designers may get it wrong by taking the above too literally; if it's a young audience, it doesn't have to be grunge; if it's an older audience, it doesn't have to be classical."
Alan Meeks (1951), British font designer

"When choosing a typeface, you must really research your brief and its character. Typefaces are visual sounds and, by using the right style, you can speak to your audience in the right tone. There is no point using Helvetica for a heavy metal band, as it simply doesn't work. I think some designers get their typography wrong simply by following others. They tend to forget who their market is and follow the crowd."
Nick Hayes, owner of Identikal Foundry

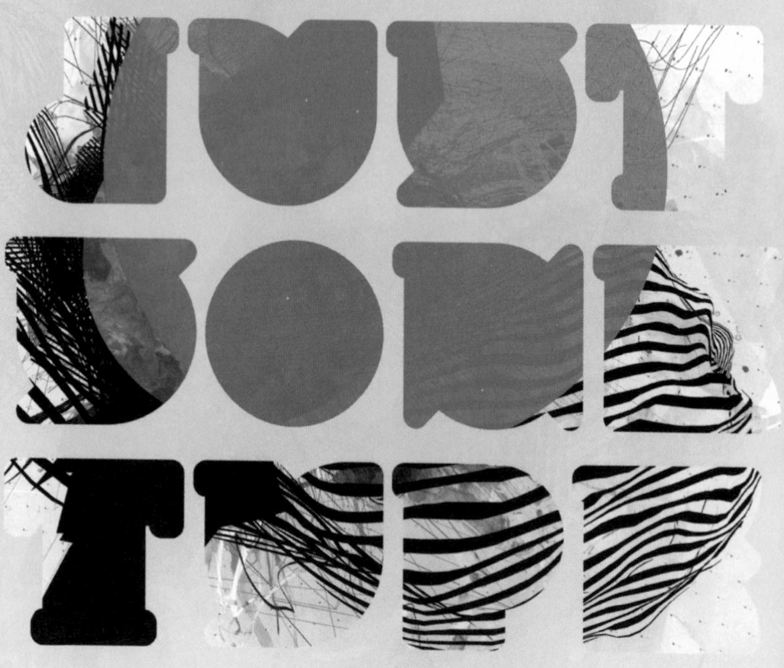
JUST
SOME
TYPE

Stick to screen fonts

rule
43

We've said it before and we'll say it again: fonts that work on paper don't necessarily work on a computer screen.

"If you're working on something such as a screen font, you have to get yourself into a certain frame of mind, because of the coarseness of the situation. What you're designing can never be perfect – you're not looking for a platonic ideal. You're looking at two lowercase 'e's and trying to decide which is less bad."
Matthew Carter (1937), British type designer

"Italic type on a screen is simply stupid. The pixel grid is square and does not allow for old typographic traditions. You can't make type light either, as you cannot have less than one pixel for a stroke. Go bold, go bigger, go color."
Erik Spiekermann (1947), German typographer and designer

"Print is a wonderful stable medium, and turns out the web is a wonderful unstable medium... Type on the web is continuously needing to be improved; over the next 2 or 3 years at least we're going to see a lot of fonts revving and re-revving to keep up with the process."
David Berlow (1954), American type designer

"I decided to take a calligraphy class to learn how to [learn calligraphy]. I learned about serif and sans-serif type-faces, about varying the space between different letter combinations, about what makes great typography great. It was beautiful. Historical. Artistically subtle in a way that science can't capture. And I found it fascinating. None of this had any hope of any practical application in my life. But 10 years later, when we were designing the first Macintosh computer, it all came back to me. And we designed it all into the Mac. It was the first computer with beautiful typography. If I had never dropped in on that single course in college, the Mac would never have had multiple typefaces or proportionally spaced fonts. And since Windows just copied the Mac, it's likely that no personal computer would have them"
Steve Jobs (1955), American businessman and co-founder of Apple and Pixar

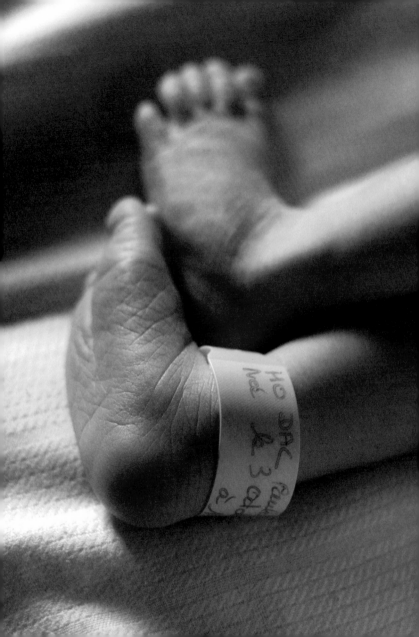

Name that type!

You've spent hours, days, months, if not years perfecting your type only to find out that designing a typeface is peanuts compared to coming up with a name for your design. Indeed, as American type designer Richard Lipton once said: "The hardest aspect of type design is naming your baby."

"The fonts I designed at Apple in 1983 – New York, Geneva, Chicago, San Francisco [originally Ransom], Monaco – were specifically designed for the screen. Most were named after Philadelphia suburbs: Paoli, Rosemont, Ardmore, and Harriton, Andy Hertz-feld's and my high school. Management insisted that the cities be upgraded to 'world-class'."
Susan Kare (1954), American graphic designer

"Some fonts which are named 'Gara-mond' have nothing to do with Gara-mond, it is rubbish. I like to call things by their proper names."
František Štorm (1966), Czech type designer

"Naming typefaces is always difficult. And then when you finally find a name you like, chances are that it is taken already or there will be some kind of trademark conflict and you have to go through the process all over again. My wife has named most of my typefaces, actually. We both riff on a theme and come up with a list of possibilities. The ones that stick are almost always the ones she came up with, though."
Cyrus Highsmith (1973), American type designer

"Never use white type on a black background."

rule
45

The rule comes courtesy of British-born advertising exec David Ogilvy, who wrote in his book *Ogilvy on Advertising* that white type on a black background doesn't work. But don't get too hung up on Ogilvy's words of wisdom; he later argued that his 'rule' was merely meant as a hint.

"I am sometimes attacked for impos-ing 'rules'. Nothing could be further from the truth. I hate rules. All I do is report on how consumers react to different stimuli. I may say to a copywriter, 'Research shows that commercials with celebrities are below average in persuading people to buy products. Are you sure you want to use a celebrity?' Call that a rule? Or I may say to an art director, 'Research suggests that if you set the copy in black type on a white background, more people will read it than if you set it in white type in a black background'. A hint, perhaps, but scarcely a rule."
David Ogilvy (1911-1999), British-born advertising executive

"In printing, dropping white type out of a dark background was once a technically precarious practice. There was the danger that the thin parts of the letters would fill in. Moreover, the difficulty of reading white against black, with the vibrations that occur on the page, often proscribe printing this way."
Steven Guarnaccia and Susan Hochbaum, designers and authors of Black & White *(2002)*

"Studies have shown that, while black type on a white background is highly legible, the same quantity of white type on a black background is harder to read."
Ina Saltz, American art director, author and professor

Keep it neutral

Opting for neutrality in design, or
'going Swiss,' is a matter of some
controversy amongst designers. In
her book *Typography Essentials,*
American designer Ina Saltz hints
at the ongoing debate, writing that
"some designers find staying neutral
to be a boring and banal exercise,"
while others perceive it as a "desir-
able characteristic."

"Simplicity and neutrality allow the text to take precedence … Helvetica is a typeface that exemplifies neutrality… Designers such as Massimo Vignelli believe that in its very neutrality, Helvetica is infinitely malleable and useful, while other designers such as Paula Scher see Helvetica as a representation of the facelessness and soullessness of big corporations and governments."
Ina Saltz, American art director and designer

"There is no such thing as a neutral typeface; a neutral typeface transmits neutrality and that is a message in itself."
Enric Jardí (1964), Spanish font and graphic designer

"Even if you choose what might be called a 'neutral' typeface, you've made a choice that tells people the message is neutral."
Erik Spiekermann and E.M. Ginger, Stop Stealing Sheep & Find Out How Type Works (2003)

The client is always right

The relationship between those who do – the designers – and those who pay – the clients – can become strained when those who pay don't let those who do, do what it is they do best… Or, in the words of American graphic designer and illustrator Von R. Glitschka (1966), "The client may be king, but he's not the art director."

"I like things that are playful; I like things that are happy; I like things that will make the client smile."
Paul Rand (1914-1996), American graphic designer

"Public recognition is important because it makes every designer more of an equal partner for the client. As long as we are considered a lower form of production service, clients will not involve us properly and will not pay us the money our work deserves."
Erik Spiekermann (1947), German typographer and designer

"The ideal client/designer relationship is one where the design is discussed from the project's start rather than being brought in as an afterthought or to jazz up a flaccid project. Type design is an activity that greatly benefits from sensitive and educated clients, as it can take an awfully long time to produce something that doesn't look like much."
Timothy Donaldson, British type designer

"In corporate communications, from letters to annual reports, the client will be more conservative, as the typeface has a different function."
Bruno Maag (1962), Swiss font designer

"The real award-winning work comes from the designers who set the trends, as well as answering their client's brief correctly."
Nick Hayes, owner of Identikal Foundry

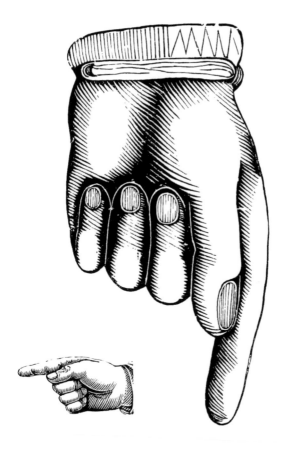

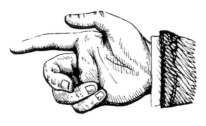

Indicate paragraphs

rule
48

Allow your readers time and room to breathe: indicate paragraphs.

———

"Dividing a text into paragraphs is a convention that only exists for written language, not for the spoken language. We make paragraphs to mark certain thematic changes but, most importantly, we help the reader by giving them a pause. Paragraphs tell us whether we have to continue on the same line or move to another, which makes them especially useful in longer texts. Choosing a type of paragraph break and structure is functional, not just aesthetic."
Enric Jardí (1964), Spanish font and graphic designer

Be creative

"For the time being technology is hampering creativity,
but hopefully not for long."

Alan Meeks (1951), British font designer

The number of rules governing the world of typography can be positively mindboggling and has the potential to stifle all creativity. Time to go back to the drawing board, let your hair down and allow the creative juices to flow.

———

"I think the creative use of typography will come from the streets. Urban artists are beginning to realize the power of type on the computer and will transfer all of their typographic ideas onto machines, rather than walls. I think the rise of urban music from the street to the charts really signifies this. Graffiti artists are really typographers, and I think they will give a fresh and new approach to type design, which is always welcome."

Nick Hayes, owner of Identikal Foundry

Designers hate Arial

All designers hate Arial, despise Comic
Sans, and adore Helvetica. Or do they?

———

"I have quite a few favorites: from our own collection I think it is InterFace. It's a sans hybrid (Grotesk and Humanist) that reads very well at small sizes and on the screen thanks to its good hinting. It's a versatile typeface family that will sit quite comfortably with a serif typeface. I do have a soft spot for Adobe's Caslon. Personally, I think it's the nicest cut around."
Bruno Maag (1962), Swiss font designer

"The most overused typeface today would have to be Helvetica."
Nick Hayes, owner of Identikal Foundry

"As designers, we hate Arial and we contrast it with Helvetica, which we think is more proper, but we need to give a long speech and point out certain formal subtleties to convince the newest converts."
Enric Jardí (1964), Spanish font and graphic designer

"I have a few strong favorites and they are all different: Franklin Gothic, Univers, Bembo, and Gill Sans. I think I have to take a desert island disc mentality and force myself to choose one, probably Gill Sans."
Timothy Donaldson, British type designer

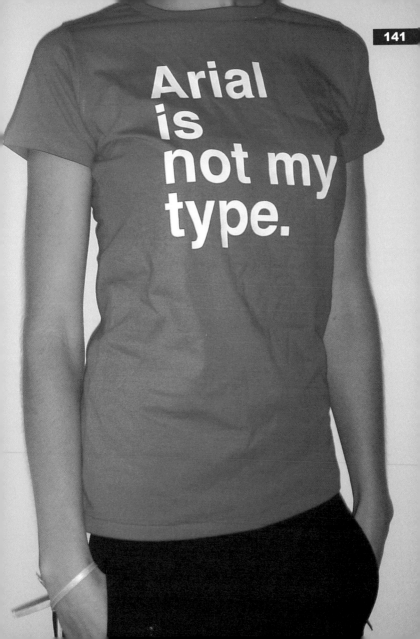

Break the rules rule **51**

No less than 50 rules have been discussed in this book. Now you know them, feel free to break them.

"The advantage of rules is that they can prevent mistakes; the disadvantage is that they can prevent discoveries."
Matthew Carter (1937), British type designer

"While the language of typography still adheres to some rules, there really aren't any standards for type designers to follow. Typographic features, such as large x-heights, wide counters, and exaggerated ascenders, are no less slaves to fashion than the perpetual changes in skirt lengths determined on Paris runways."
Erik Spiekermann (1947), German typographer and designer

"Rules are good. Break them."
Tibor Kalman (1949-1999), Hungarian-born American graphic designer

"Never embark on a project without a rule. But be open to breaking that rule when necessary."
Enric Jardí (1964), Spanish font and graphic designer

"Rules can be broken – but never ignored."
David Jury, author of About Face: Reviving the Rules of Typography (2002)

"Typography and letters are meant to convey information. I break that rule. The work is titled 'WHAT EVER' and that is exactly what it says, but the letters in my drawings have such an abstract shape that they conjure up a feeling instead of conveying information. Legibility is gone but once you recognize the letters that the shapes represent, you're able to read the work."
Louis Reith, Dutch graphic designer, on the work pictured on the left

"Type design becomes experimental when the traditional rules are broken."
Adam Hayes, owner of Identikal Foundry

CONTRIBUTORS

1 DTM_INC
(www.behance.net/dtm_inc)

2 Oded Ezer
(www.odedezer.com)

3 Stefano Joker Lionett
(www.loveleft.com)

4 Petar Pavlov
(www.behance.net/petar_pavlov)

5 Paul Tomlin (cc)
(www.flickr.com/paultomlin)

6 visualpanic / Lali Masriera (cc)
(www.visualpanic.net)

7 Jan Tik (cc)
(www.flickr.com/jantik)

21 Branislav S. Cirkovic
(www.typoflat.com)

22 Carolin Nagel
(www.not-my-type.com)

23 Jeroen Disch.
(www.disch.nl)

24 Louis Reith
(www.louisreith.com)

25 ODHD / olivier hodac (cc)
(www.flickr.com/hodac)

26 Julian Hansen
(www.julianhansen.com)

27 _Nec / Szabolcs Toth (cc)
(www.flickr.com/necccc)

28 DoubleM2 (cc)
(www.flickr.com/photos/49879584@N00)

29 davitydave / David Lytle (cc)
(www.flickr.com/dlytle)

30 Laura Jooren
(www.laurajooren.wordpress.com)

31 Sander van Loon
(www.who-are-we.com)

32 Charlotte Lokin
(www.charlottelokin.com)

INDEX BY SUBJECT

INDEX BY NAME

Also available

**Never Use White Type on a Black Background
And 50 other Ridiculous Design Rules**

"One of the most fun and quirky books one can read about rules in the world of fashion and design. Great for a laugh and to challenge your thinking and pre-conceptions as a designer."
- *Design Indaba Magazine*

ISBN 978 90 6369 207 0

**Never Leave the House Naked
And 50 other Ridiculous Fashion Rules**

"The book is neatly designed. Small format, great graphics and plenty of illustrations commissioned to talented young graphic designers."
- *We Make Money Not Art*

ISBN 978 90 6369 214 8

**The Medium is the Message
And 50 other Ridiculous Advertising Rules**

"The book light-heartedly pokes fun at statements that, either for good or bad, have become clichéd principles of advertising."
- *Dezeen*

ISBN 978 90 6369 215 5

**Never Use Pop Up Windows
And 50 other Ridiculous Web Rules**

ISBN 978 90 6369 217 9

BISPUBLISHERS
www.bispublishers.nl

Thanks to:
Premsela, Dutch Platform for Design and Fashion (www.premsela.org)
Lemon scented tea (www.lemonscentedtea.com)